Dinosaurs and more Dinosaurs

by M. JEAN CRAIG

Pictures by GEORGE SOLONEVICH

SCHOLASTIC BOOK SERVICES

NEW YORK • LONDON • RICHMOND HILL, ONTARIO

The author and publisher acknowledge with thanks the valuable assistance given by Georg Zappler of the American Museum of Natural History, New York City. Mr. Zappler checked not only the text, but also the illustrations.

Because the dinosaur paintings in this book are such a departure from conventional illustration, we have asked Mr. Zappler to comment on them from a specialist's point of view.

The fresh and original illustrations by George Solonevich reflect a great gift for bringing to life creatures now long dead and known only from scattered fossil remains.

As with all such reconstructions, much of the detailed anatomy and over-all proportions are in the realm of the educated guess. Skin texture and color, and even bodily poses, can only be conjectured in many instances.

In spite of these difficulties, the artist has given the public a breath-taking view of the dominant inhabitants of our earth some 100 million years ago.

GEORG ZAPPLER
American Museum of
Natural History
New York City

An expanded version of this book is published in a hardcover edition by Four Winds Press, a division of Scholastic, and is available through your local bookstore or directly from Four Winds Press, 50 West 44th St., New York, N.Y. 10036.

4th printing .... November 1968

Printed in the U.S.A.

Contents

Many, many millions of years ago, the world was a wetter place than it is today. Much of the land that is now meadow and hillside was covered with lakes and great seas and flat, muddy marshes.

The weather was warmer than it is now, too, all over the world. It was warm even near the North Pole and the South Pole. And it stayed warm all year long.

It was in this wet, warm world that the dinosaurs lived.

For over a hundred million years there were

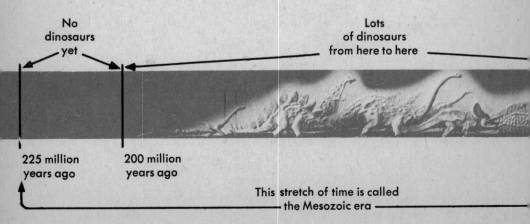

No dinosaurs yet

Lots of dinosaurs from here to here

225 million years ago

200 million years ago

This stretch of time is called the Mesozoic era

dinosaurs in every part of the world, wherever there was land for them to walk on. And then, about seventy million years ago, the last dinosaurs died out. They died out a long, long time before there were any men in the world.

No man ever hunted a dinosaur.

No dinosaur ever hunted a man.

No man ever saw a dinosaur when it was alive.

Then how do we know that there were dinosaurs?

And how do we know what they were like?

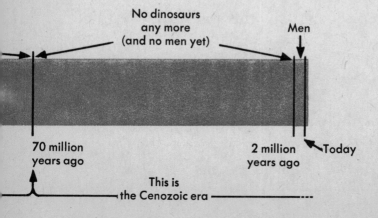

No dinosaurs any more (and no men yet)

Men

70 million years ago

2 million years ago

Today

This is the Cenozoic era

How we know
about dinosaurs

When dinosaurs died, their bodies sank down into the mud or sand. As years passed, some of their bones and teeth and bits of skin turned slowly to stone or mineral. Sometimes the eggs of dinosaurs turned to stone, too. Bones and teeth and eggs that have turned to stone are called *fossils*.

Dinosaurs often left footprints in the mud where they walked. Sometimes this mud dried up and became stone, and we can still see the fossil footprints.

Wherever we find dinosaur footprints or other dinosaur fossils, we can say, "Dinosaurs lived here."

We can tell how big dinosaurs were by the size of their bones and their footprints.

We can figure out what dinosaurs ate by the kind of teeth they had. Some ate hard plants and some ate soft plants. Some ate small animals and insects. Some ate other dinosaurs!

And when we study dinosaur bones and fit them together, we can guess how dinosaurs moved about. We can even guess what they looked like.

Strong sharp teeth for tearing chunks of meat

Rough tooth plates for grinding hard plants

Little blunt teeth for mashing soft plants

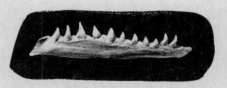

Little sharp teeth for cutting bits of meat

When the dinosaurs lived

The men who study the past have divided all of Earth's time into parts. Each part is called an *era*. The dinosaurs lived in the *Mesozoic era*. (That is pronounced mezz-o-**zoe**-ik).

The Mesozoic era was 155 million years long. This era has been divided again, into three *periods*. The dinosaurs appeared during the first period, and they lived all through the second and third.

During the last ten or twenty million years of the Mesozoic era, all the dinosaurs died out.

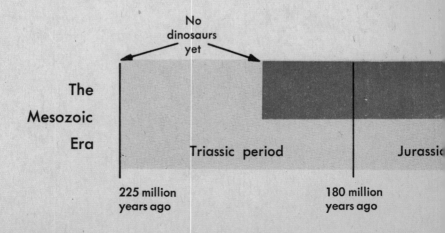

No dinosaurs yet

The Mesozoic Era

Triassic period

Jurassic

225 million years ago

180 million years ago

**The Triassic (try-ass-ik) period
was 45 million years long.**

Dinosaurs first appeared in this period. There were not many kinds of dinosaurs.

**The Jurassic (joo-rass-ik) period
was 45 million years long.**

There were many more kinds of dinosaurs. The biggest plant-eating giants lived in this period.

**The Cretaceous (kre-tay-shus) period
was 65 million years long.**

There were more kinds of dinosaurs than ever before. The biggest, fiercest meat-eaters lived in this period.

eriod

Cretaceous period

135 million
years ago

70 million
years ago

Dinosaur ancestors

The dinosaurs were a kind of *reptile*. (The snakes and crocodiles and lizards and turtles that live today are reptiles too.) Before the reptiles came along, all of the animals who lived in the world were water animals. The reptiles were the first animals who could live on dry land all of the time. All the reptiles could breathe air, and they laid eggs with shells, which could hatch on dry land.

There were other kinds of reptiles in the world for a long time before there were dinosaurs. Some of these early reptiles are called *thecodonts* (**theek**-o-donts). The thecodonts were the ancestors of all the dinosaurs.

In some ways, the thecodonts were different from other reptiles. Their bones were light and

10

thin, and often hollow. They ran about on their strong back legs. Their front legs were small, and the thecodonts used them like hands to catch other small reptiles and insects, for food. They were about 6 feet long, a little shorter than your bed.

The very first dinosaurs were not very big, either. They ate meat; they ran around on their back legs; they used their front feet like hands.

Later on there were hundreds of different kinds of dinosaurs, of all sizes and shapes. But the first dinosaurs were very much like the thecodonts.

The first dinosaurs

The Triassic period

During the Triassic period, some of the land became drier than it had been before. Some of the water was beginning to run off into the rivers and oceans. There were still many swamps and lakes and seas, but there were more plains and jungles than there had been earlier. There were even some volcanoes.

The first dinosaurs appeared, we think, after the middle of the Triassic period. They were probably

all little meat-eaters, like their thecodont ancestors.

But by the end of the Triassic period, there were new kinds of dinosaurs.

Some were still like the very first ones — small, light meat-eaters who walked on their hind legs.

But some were big, heavy meat-eaters who walked on their hind legs.

And one kind of big, heavy dinosaur began to eat plants. These new dinosaurs used all four legs for walking.

On the next pages you will find some of the dinosaurs who lived in the first dinosaur period.

Coelophysis (see-lo-fise-iss)

Coelophysis was about 10 feet long, but he was only as heavy as an eight-year-old-boy. This is because his bones were thin and hollow, like a bird's bones.

Coelophysis ran about lightly and swiftly on his hind legs. His front legs had fingers and claws. His sharp teeth had rough edges, like a saw. It must have been easy for him to catch smaller animals and tear them into bite-size pieces.

Skeletons of these dinosaurs have been found in New Mexico. Some rocks in Connecticut show fossil footprints that might have been made by Coelophysis. Or perhaps they were made by another meat-eater called Podokesaurus, who looked very much like Coelophysis.

Coelophysis

Podokesaurus (po-doke-ee-saw-rus)

Teratosaurus (ter-rat-o-saw-rus)

One kind of big meat-eating dinosaur who lived in the first dinosaur period was called Teratosaurus. He was longer than a car (20 feet), and had solid bones and a big, heavy head and a thick, strong tail. He weighed half a ton — as much as 20 eight-year-old boys all together.

Teratosaurus walked on his back legs. His front feet had a big hooked claw on each thumb, and his teeth were like sharp knives.

Claws and teeth like that must have been very useful when dinnertime came along.

These dinosaurs lived in Germany, and probably in other parts of the world too. Some scientists think they died out at the end of the Triassic period.

Plateosaurus (plat-ee-o-saw-rus)

Plateosaurus couldn't have torn up meat with his blunt teeth, so we know that he must have eaten plants.

Plateosaurus is the earliest kind of large plant-eater we have found. He was the ancestor of the plant-eating giants who came along later. (Plateosaurus was about 20 feet long, which is rather small for a giant!)

These dinosaurs could walk on their strong back legs, but often they went on all fours. They dragged their heavy tails on the ground behind them.

Plateosaurus fossils have been found in Germany, and other dinosaurs like them lived in South Africa, in China, and in North America.

Yaleosaurus (yale-ee-o-saw-rus)

Yaleosaurus was one of the early dinosaurs who ate plants. He walked some of the time on his back legs, but some of the time he came down on all fours. Perhaps he did this so he could reach low plants more easily.

These dinosaurs were 7 or 8 feet long. Some of them lived in the valley of the Connecticut River.

Another name for Yaleosaurus is Anchi-saurus (**ank-i-saw**-rus).

Other Triassic animals

During the Triassic period, there were many other kinds of animal life along with the dinosaurs. There were no birds yet, but there were some insects, and there may have been the first tiny, furry, warm-blooded animals called mammals.

Most of the land animals were reptiles.

Little reptiles something like lizards darted about on high ground.

Big reptiles shaped like crocodiles, but as long as a bus, splashed in the shallow water near the beaches.

Some reptiles now had hard shells — they were the first turtles.

Some kinds of reptiles could swim in the water, like their fishy ancestors, although they breathed air just like all the other reptiles.

More dinosaurs
The Jurassic period

The Jurassic period began 180 million years ago, and lasted for 45 million years.

The weather was as warm as it had been earlier, and the world was still a very wet place. Shallow seas still covered the western part of North America. Much of Europe was covered by ocean, too. Here and there small islands poked up out of the water.

At the edges of the seas there were muddy swamps, thick with water-plants. On higher land there were large green ferns and trees like palm trees. It was a wonderful world for animals to live in, especially for dinosaurs.

There were more kinds of dinosaurs now.

There were still the small meat-eaters. There were new kinds of very big meat-eaters. And there were some new and *enormous* plant-eating giants, whose ancestors were the plant-eaters of the Triassic period.

In this second dinosaur period, we begin to find different kinds of middle-sized plant-eaters too, not even related to the plant-eating giants.

Some of these new plant-eaters walked on their hind legs. They were the ancestors of many more kinds of plant-eaters who lived later on.

Other new plant-eaters walked on four feet. They had flat plates growing up from the skin on their backs. This kind of plant-eater died out around the end of the Jurassic period.

On the following pages you can see what the Jurassic dinosaurs were like.

Ornitholestes (or-nith-o-less-teez)

This name means "bird-stealer," and these dinosaurs may have been quick enough to catch a bird. But most of the time they probably ate insects and eggs and other small animals.

They were 5 or 6 feet tall (only about as tall as a man). They were light and graceful, like their ancestors who lived in the Triassic period. Their small front legs each had three long fingers, to snatch with, and their teeth were very sharp.

There are Ornitholestes fossils in Wyoming.

You could have held Compsognathus in your two hands. He was just the size of a small cat. He was, in fact, the very smallest kind of dinosaur we know about.

This dinosaur was a meat-eater, with sharp teeth and a little, bird-like head.

His little, bird-like bones were found in Germany.

Ceratosaurus (ser-rat-o-saw-rus)

The *Cerato-* that you see in this name comes from a Greek word that means "horn," and this was the only meat-eating dinosaur that had a horn on his nose.

These dinosaurs were about 17 feet long — not as big as some other big meat-eaters. But they were heavy, and they could move quickly. The little animals had to run fast to get away from Ceratosaurus.

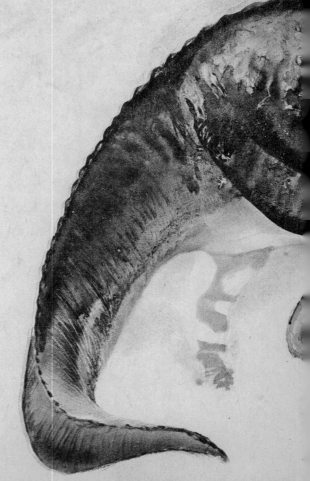

Megalosaurus (meg-a-lo-saw-rus)

Megalosaurus was one of the big meat-eaters. He was over 20 feet long, and his skull and his teeth were enormous.

The bones of Megalosaurus were first found in England in 1824, nearly 150 years ago. No one knew at that time just what this big beast was, or just how long ago it had lived, so it was given a name which means simply "big reptile." Now, of course, we have learned a lot more about dinosaurs.

Other Megalosaurus fossils have been found in Africa.

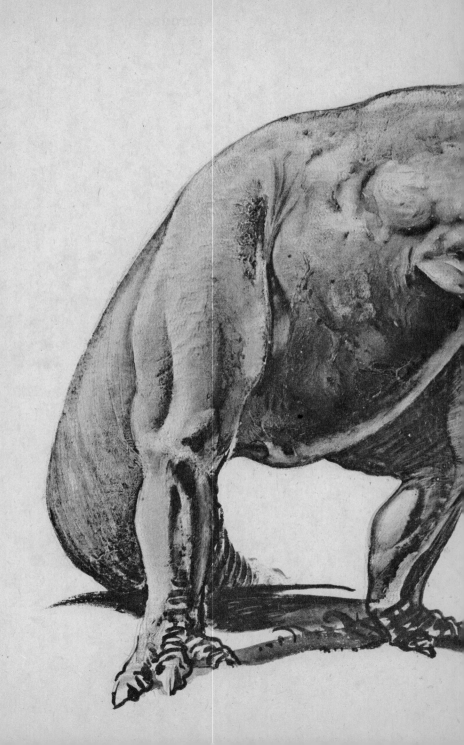

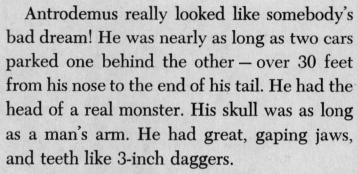

Antrodemus (an-tro-dee-mus)

Antrodemus really looked like somebody's bad dream! He was nearly as long as two cars parked one behind the other — over 30 feet from his nose to the end of his tail. He had the head of a real monster. His skull was as long as a man's arm. He had great, gaping jaws, and teeth like 3-inch daggers.

Antrodemus had strong back legs, like the legs of a giant bird. He could run across dry ground at high speed. His front legs were too short to help hold up his body. But each front foot had three large claws which were very useful for attack.

These dinosaurs could kill and eat even the very biggest reptiles. Apatosaurus (a-**pat**-o-saw-rus) bones have been found with Antrodemus toothmarks on them.

Antrodemus used to be called Allosaurus (**al**-lo-**saw**-rus).

31

Camarasaurus (cam-are-a-saw-rus)

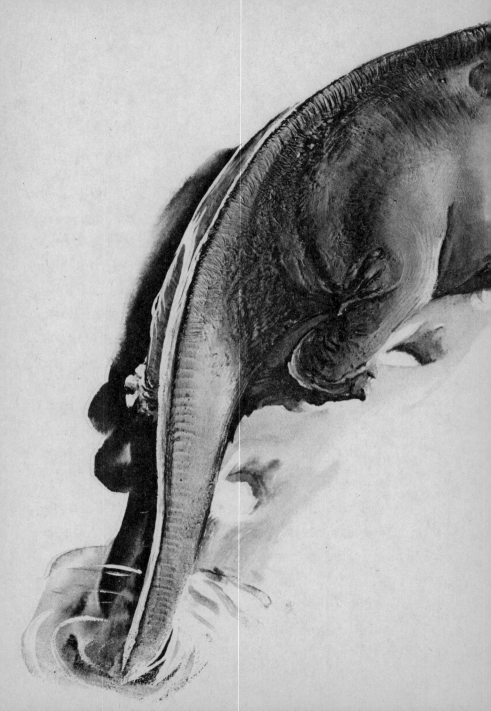

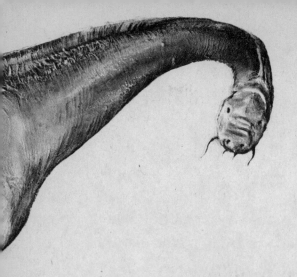

In the Jurassic period, there were a great many new kinds of giant plant-eaters splashing about in marshes and swamps all over the world. Camarasaurus was one of the smallest of the new giants, but even so, he was about 50 feet long.

These dinosaurs never stood up on their hind legs; they plopped around in the mud on four flat feet.

Fossils of Camarasaurus have been found in North America. They probably lived in other places too.

The ancestor of these new giant plant-eaters was Plateosaurus (**plat**-ee-o-**saw**-rus), who lived earlier in Triassic times. (Read about Plateosaurus on page 18.)

Cetiosaurus (see-tee-o-saw-rus)

The bones of Cetiosaurus were discovered in England over a hundred years ago. The name means "whale-reptile," and these dinosaurs *were* as big as whales. They were about 60 feet long.

Like all the giant plant-eaters, Cetiosaurus had dull little teeth and ate green water-plants.

These dinosaurs lived in Africa, as well as in England. We think they lived in other parts of the world, too.

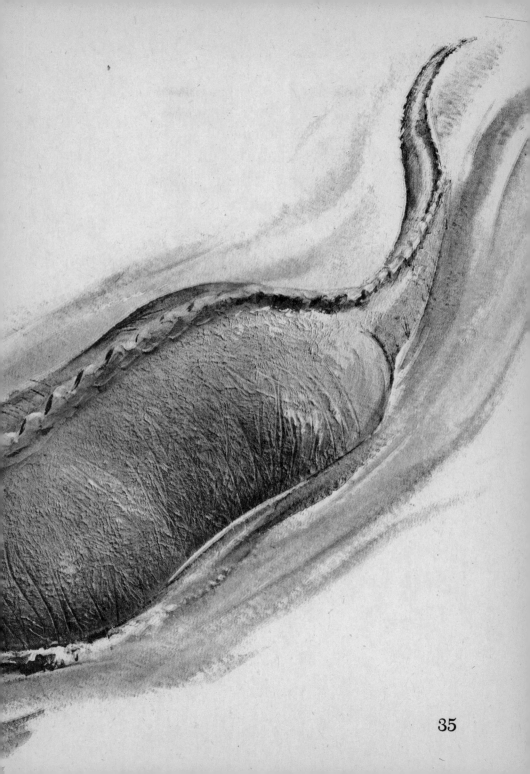

Apatosaurus (a-pat-o-saw-rus)

Many people call this dinosaur *Brontosaurus* (**bron**-to-**saw**-rus), which means "thunder-reptile." It is possible that the ground did thunder and shake when these dinosaurs walked across it. They weighed 40 tons, and they were about 70 feet long. (That's as long as two big city busses, one behind the other.) Apatosaurus had a small head, though, and his brain was only as big as man's fist.

These huge animals lived along the edges of the lakes that used to cover Wyoming. They had little, spoon-shaped teeth, and ate water-plants. They probably waded into deeper water to get away from Antrodemus when one of those dreadful beasts appeared.

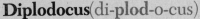

Diplodocus(di-plod-o-cus)

Diplodocus was not as heavy as Apatosaurus, because so much of him was a thin snaky neck and a thin snaky tail. But he was the *longest* dinosaur we have ever found. He was about 80 feet long, and that's as long as four big cars lined up waiting for the light to turn green.

These dinosaurs splashed through the marshes and lakes of what is now the western

part of the United States. They chewed up soft water-plants with teeth shaped like short pencil stubs.

Diplodocus had nose openings on the very top of his skull. He could walk along the bottom of a deep lake, and still breathe very nicely without poking his whole head out of the water.

Dicraeosaurus(di-cree-o-saw-rus)

A dinosaur who was very much like Diplodocus lived in East Africa. He is called Dicraeosaurus.

Brachiosaurus (brack-ee-o-saw-rus)

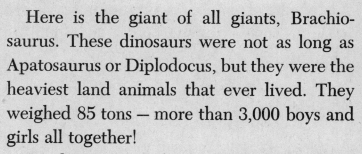

Here is the giant of all giants, Brachiosaurus. These dinosaurs were not as long as Apatosaurus or Diplodocus, but they were the heaviest land animals that ever lived. They weighed 85 tons — more than 3,000 boys and girls all together!

Brachiosaurus was the only giant plant-eater whose front legs were longer than his back legs. Because of this, he could hold his head high up in the air. If there had been a three-story building around when these dinosaurs lived, they could have peeked down the chimney without even stretching.

Brachiosaurus could look for food in deep water, like Diplodocus. When he wanted to breathe, he just had to stand up straight, because his nose was way up on the top of his skull, in a little dome.

These *giant* giants lived in East Africa.

Scelidosaurus (skel-lid-o-saw-rus)

Some plant-eating dinosaurs who appeared in the Jurassic period were not a bit like the giant plant-eaters. They were not even related to them.

Scelidosaurus is the earliest one of these "different" plant-eaters that we know about. And we have learned about him from part of a single fossil skeleton found in a cliff in England.

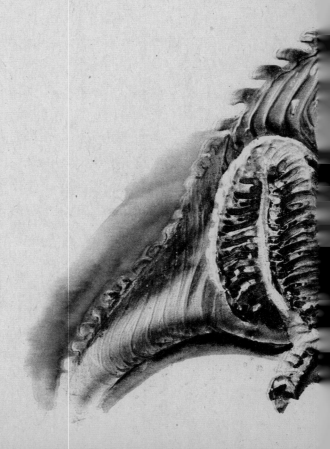

Scelidosaurus was 13 feet long — about as long as two beds. He had broad feet, a small head, and weak jaws. His neck, body, and tail had rows of short, pointed plates that stood straight up in the air. He would have been a very nasty, scratchy mouthful for any meateater.

Stegosaurus(steg-o-saw-rus)

Stegosaurus had bony plates on his back, like a row of little sails, and sharp spikes on his tail.

The front legs of Stegosaurus were so short that his hips humped high in the air. He was longer than a car — 20 feet — but he had a little head and a small beak of a mouth and a tiny, tiny brain. His brain was only as big as a prune, so we don't think Stegosaurus was a very smart dinosaur.

These plant-eaters lived all over the world. Their bones or their plates have been found in the state of Wyoming, and also in England, in Asia, in Africa, and in South America.

Many kinds of Jurassic dinosaurs lived in later times, too, but Stegosaurus died out when the Jurassic period ended.

Dacentrurus (day-sen-troo-rus)

Dacentrurus was very much like Stegosaurus, and lived in many parts of Europe. Some fossil eggs found in Portugal may be Dacentrurus eggs. This dinosaur has also been called Omosaurus (**o**-mo-**saw**-rus).

Camptosaurus (camp-to-saw-rus)

These dinosaurs lived late in the Jurassic period, in the western part of North America.

Plant-eaters like Camptosaurus were the ancestors of many different new kinds of plant-eaters who appeared later on.

Camptosaurus moved about slowly on two legs. He probably came down on all fours to eat, like a kangaroo. (But he couldn't hop like a kangaroo.) Scientists have found Camptosaurus skeletons 4 to 15 feet long.

These dinosaurs had no good way to defend themselves. They must often have made fine meals for the big meat-eaters.

Other Jurassic animals

Other new kinds of animals lived in the Jurassic period, along with the new kinds of dinosaurs.

There were new kinds of reptiles in this period. The first lizards and the first crocodiles appeared, and there may have been snakes.

In the water there were big sea-turtles and other new swimming reptiles.

One new kind of reptile now had wings, something like a bat's wings. These reptiles could fly.

There were frogs in the Jurassic period that were like today's frogs. Late in the Jurassic period the first real birds appeared, with the first real feathers.

And we have found some fossil remains of small, warm-blooded Jurassic mammals. There must have been many of them.

The last dinosaurs

The Cretaceous period

The Cretaceous period began 135 million years ago, and it lasted for 65 million years.

When it began, most of the world was still warm all year long. We know, from fossil plants we have found, that there were palm trees growing in Alaska at that time.

But then changes began to take place. Much more water drained from the land, leaving dry mountains and plains where there had been seas and marshes before. It began to be warmer in the summer and colder in the winter.

A new kind of plant life appeared. If you could take a walk in the woods near the end of the Cretaceous period, you would feel quite at home.

You would see maple and walnut and oak trees, poplars and willows and pines. And you would see flowering bushes and plants. (There had never been flowers before.)

In the Cretaceous period, there were more dinosaurs than ever. There were still small, swift meat-eaters. There were still big, heavy meat-eaters. The biggest meat-eater that ever walked on earth lived in the last dinosaur period.

There weren't many of the giant plant-eaters left. But there were dozens of new kinds of smaller ones.

There were new kinds of plant-eaters with horns.

There were new kinds of plant-eaters with heavy coverings of bone, like armor.

And there were many new kinds of plant-eaters that we call the "duck-bills."

You will find many of these wonderful dinosaurs in the following pages.

Iguanodon (ig-wan-o-don)

The first dinosaur fossil ever found was a piece of a big tooth. It was picked up by an English doctor who was out for a walk. He thought it looked like the tooth of an American lizard called *Iguana*, except that it was bigger. He named the animal it came from Iguanodon, which means "iguana-tooth."

Later, Iguanodon teeth and bones turned up in another part of England. Then whole Iguanodon skeletons were uncovered in a coal mine in Belgium. There are fossil foot-

prints of Iguanodon in Germany and in China, and in some other places. These active plant-eaters probably lived all over the world.

They were about 30 feet long, and stood tall enough to look through the bedroom window of a two-story house. They walked, most of the time, on their hind legs, and used their front feet like hands. Instead of thumbs, Iguanodon had short, sharp spikes, but we don't know what these spikes were for.

These dinosaurs lived very early in the Cretaceous period. Their ancestors may have been the Jurassic dinosaurs called Campto-saurus (**camp**-to-**saw**-rus). (You can see a picture of Camptosaurus on page 48.)

Hypsilophodon (hip-si-loff-o-don)

These were the smallest plant-eating dinosaurs, only about 5 feet long. They lived at the same time as Iguanodon, early in the last dinosaur period. Hypsilophodon bones have been found on the seashore of an island near England.

These dinosaurs may have sometimes walked on all fours, and some people think they could climb trees. Their front feet each had five long, strong fingers, which certainly would have been helpful for climbing.

Hypsilophodon had a beaky mouth. He had teeth along the sides of his jaws, but only a few teeth in front.

Thescelosaurus (thess-el-o-saw-rus)

Thescelosaurus was another harmless plant-eater. He was about 9 feet tall. The bones of his tail could lock together. This made the tail stiff, and may have helped Thescelosaurus keep his balance as he ran about quickly on his thin hind legs.

Polacanthus (poll-a-can-thus)

Here is one of the early armored dinosaurs, and he certainly wears lots of kinds of protection! He has seven or eight pairs of spines down his back, *and* plates standing up from his tail, *and* a bony shield over his hips! It would be very surprising if any of the giant meat-eaters had much appetite for Polacanthus.

These dinosaurs were low, heavy, and about 14 feet long. Their little blunt teeth show that they ate plants. They lived in England.

Syrmosaurus (sir-mo-saw-rus)

These armored plant-eaters tramped about solidly on all four feet. They were about the same size as Polacanthus. They lived early in the Cretaceous period in Mongolia, which is part of Asia.

Psittacosaurus (sit-a-ko-saw-rus)

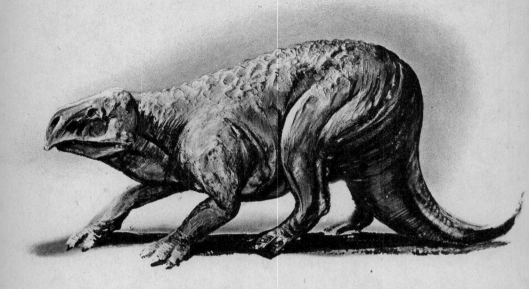

Psittacosaurus means "parrot-reptile," and it isn't hard to see how this dinosaur got his name.

He came along *after* the early plant-eaters who walked on two legs, but *before* the late plant-eaters who walked on all fours and had horns. He was probably related to both kinds. Psittacosaurus was only as tall as a man.

These dinosaurs lived in Mongolia and China.

Pachycephalosaurus (pack-ee-seff-a-lo-saw-rus)

In the town of Ekalaka, Montana, the high school students like to hunt for dinosaur fossils. One day they came across a very ugly, knobby fossil head. No one had ever seen one like it before. No one since then has ever found another one like it, either.

The top of the fossil head was a solid chunk of bone, 9 inches thick. This dinosaur was given a name that means "thick-headed reptile."

Although Pachycephalosaurus has such a very long name, he was probably one of the smaller dinosaurs. No one has ever found a body to fit the head, so we can't be sure of his size.

He was a plant-eater, and scientists think he was related to the duck-billed dinosaurs.

There were other "thick-heads" with smaller heads, called Stegoceras (**steg**-o-**serr**-is). They lived in Canada and in Eastern Asia.

Anatosaurus (an-at-o-saw-rus)

These duck-billed dinosaurs had a flat, wide mouth that really did look like a duck's beak. They lived in North America and in Europe and Asia — perhaps in Japan, too.

Anatosaurus was about 30 feet long, and very heavy. His front legs were nearly as strong as his back legs. He had webbed fingers and toes and a flat-sided, strong tail, so we are sure he was a good swimmer. He probably scooped up plants from the bottom of shallow water, like a duck, and then swam off into deep water if a big meat-eater passed by.

The flat beak of Anatosaurus was toothless, but his side jaws, further back, had more than 1,000 tiny grinding teeth, packed together into tight rows. He could grind up very tough plants.

Some fossil skin of Anatosaurus was found

in Wyoming. It is like leather with little hard bumps all over it.

We know almost everything about Anatosaurus, except what color he was.

Some dinosaur skeletons found without heads have been called Hadrosaurus (**had**-ro-**saw**-rus) skeletons, and some dinosaur teeth have been called Trachodon (**track**-o-don) teeth. But now scientists think these bones and teeth are from dinosaurs pretty much the same as Anatosaurus.

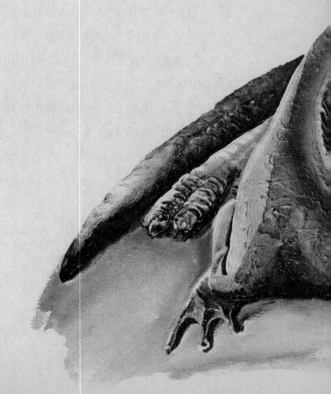

Corythosaurus (co-rith-o-saw-rus)

Corythosaurus was a close relative of Anatosaurus. He was about the same size, and he was a plant-eater, and he could swim, too.

Corythosaurus had a bony crest on top of his head that looked a little like a helmet. (Corythosaurus means "reptile-with-a-helmet.")

Prosaurolophus (pro-saw-rol-o-fuss)

There were other dinosaurs with crests on their heads. Some crests were round knobs. Some looked like real horns. But all these crests were really just the dinosaur's nose bones, pushed up under the skin into different shapes.

Some dinosaurs had solid crests. Prosaurolophus had a low, bony bump above his eyes.

Saurolophus (saw-**rol**-o-fuss)

Parasaurolophus (pa-ra-saw-**rol**-o-fuss)

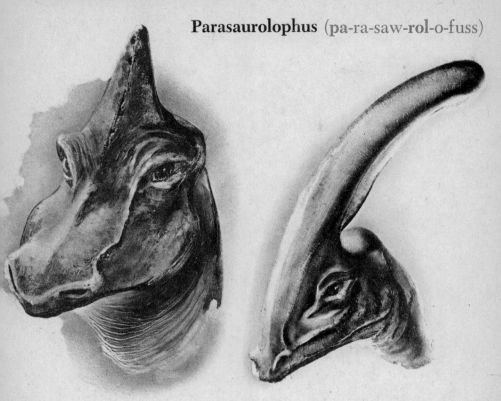

Saurolophus had solid nose bones too, but they were the shape of a single long spike.

Some dinosaurs had hollow crests. When the dinosaur breathed, air went from his nostrils through tubes in his crest, and then down into his lungs. The crest of Parasaurolophus was a long hollow tube that curved way back over his neck. It was twice as long as his head.

Lambeosaurus (lam-bee-o-saw-rus)

Lambeosaurus had a hollow crest, shaped like the blade of a hatchet. The helmet-crest of Corythosaurus was hollow, too.

The crested dinosaurs all had very sharp eyes and very good ears. Breathing air through the tubes in the crests may have helped them smell especially well, too.

Many of the crested dinosaurs lived in Canada. Their fossils have also been found in other parts of the world.

Ankylosaurus (an-kile-o-saw-rus)

Paleoscincus (pay-lee-o-skink-us)

Ankylosaurus and Paleoscincus were two armored dinosaurs. The heavy plates of bone covering their skin protected them from the big meat-eaters.

These two kinds of dinosaurs lived in North America, near the end of the Cretaceous period.

Ankylosaurus and Paleoscincus were very much alike.

They were both 15 to 18 feet long — about as long as a car. They both had short, heavy legs, and walked with their small heads down low. They both had teeth like tiny beads, and could have eaten only the very softest plants.

But they were not *exactly* alike.

Ankylosaurus

Paleoscincus

Ankylosaurus had two sharp points on his head, and a great bony knob on the end of his tail. He may have used this knob to swat a meat-eater who was thinking of killing and eating him.

Paleoscincus had a smooth head, something like a turtle's, and sharp spines near his shoulders. He had spines along the edges of his tail, too, but no knob at the end.

Protoceratops (pro-toe-serr-a-tops)

Many of the plant-eaters who lived at the end of the Cretaceous period had bony shields, or frills, on their heads, and horns as well.

Protoceratops was one of the first of these horned dinosaurs, although he didn't really have horns — just the bony shield. He was a little dinosaur, only 6 feet long. His head was nearly as big as the rest of his body, and his shield went way back over his shoulders.

The front of his beaked little mouth had no teeth, but there were teeth along the sides of his jaws.

Protoceratops fossils were first discovered in Mongolia, in 1922. And Protoceratops eggs — hundreds of them — were found in sand nests along with the bones. Some of the eggs had tiny, unhatched dinosaurs inside.

The ancestor of Protoceratops may have been Psittacosaurus (**sit**-a-ko-**saw**-rus), whose picture is on page 58.

Monoclonius (mo-no-clone-ee-us)

Monoclonius appeared later than Protoceratops, and was three times as big. He was a
plant-eater too, and he lived in North America.

He had a horn on his nose like a rhinoceros.
His short bony frill had bumps along the
edge, and little hooks.

Styracosaurus (stee-rak-o-saw-rus)

Another horned plant-eater was Styraco-
saurus. He lived in North America at the same
time as Monoclonius, and was about the same
size — 18 feet long. He had the same kind of
nose horn, but his shield, or frill, had very long
spikes sticking out of it in all directions, with
two extra-long ones at the back edge.

Chasmosaurus (kaz-mo-saw-rus)

Chasmosaurus was 18 or 20 feet long. He
had a longer bony shield than Monoclonius,
and there were big holes in the bone, covered
with skin. The horn on his nose was short; the
horns above his eyes were long. He was another North American plant-eater.

Pentaceratops (pen-ta-serr-a-tops)

This horned plant-eater was over 20 feet long, and lived in North America and in Asia late in the Cretaceous period.

Pentaceratops had a very long shield, with holes in the bone. And he had two very long horns above his eyes, and a fine nose horn, and two more horns on the corners of his jaw. That makes five horns altogether, and Pentaceratops means "five-horns-on-the-face."

Triceratops (try-serr-a-tops)

Triceratops (whose name means "three-horns-on-the-face") was one of the last and one of the biggest of the horned plant-eaters. He was 24 feet long — four times the size of little Protoceratops.

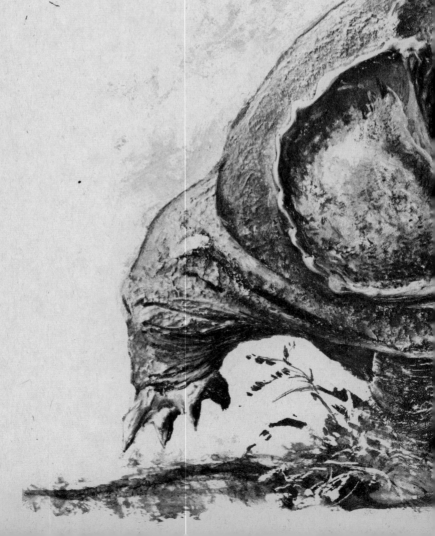

Triceratops had two enormous horns pointing forward like two great, heavy spears. We think he used them like spears too, to defend himself.

These dinosaurs lived in North America.

Hypselosaurus (hip-sel-o-saw-rus)

Hypselosaurus was one kind of giant plant-eater who lived in the third dinosaur period. (Many of the giant plant-eaters, like Apatosaurus, had died out by the end of the second dinosaur period.)

Hypselosaurus was 40 feet long and weighed about 10 tons.

Eggs of these dinosaurs have been found in France. They are not much bigger than a big potato. And the baby Hypselosaurus, just hatched, didn't weigh much more than a kitten. How long it must have taken for a baby Hypselosaurus to grow up!

Ornithomimus was about three times as tall as you are. He lived in North America and in Asia, and he was related to the small meat-eaters. He could run very fast on his hind legs, and he used his front legs for pulling and tearing, just like any meat-eater.

But his neck was longer than most meat-eaters' necks. And he had a beak like a bird's, with no teeth at all, so he couldn't have chewed meat. He may have gulped down small, soft animals and insects, and perhaps he ate fruit, too. It is possible that what he really liked best were the eggs of other dinosaurs. The fossil of a dinosaur like Ornithomimus was once found in a nest of Protoceratops eggs.

Ornithomimus means "like a bird." Some of these dinosaurs have also been called Struthiomimus (**strooth**-ee-o-**my**-mus), which means "like an ostrich."

Gorgosaurus (gore-go-saw-rus)

Most of the dinosaurs living in the Cretaceous period were plant-eaters. But there were meat-eaters, too. There were little meat-eaters as there had always been, and also some very big ones.

The giant dinosaurs called Megalosaurus, who lived earlier, in the Jurassic period, still roamed across the land. Later, in the Cretaceous period, there was also the monster Gorgosaurus, about 30 feet long. He tramped about in North America on his great three-toed hind feet, hunting the plant-eaters.

Gorgosaurus was probably the ancestor of the dinosaurs called Tyrannosaurus Rex.

Tyrannosaurus Rex (tie-ran-o-saw-rus rex)

Tyrannosaurus Rex means "king of the tyrant reptiles," and this giant looks like a king indeed, and perhaps a tyrant, too. He was the biggest meat-eating land animal that ever lived, and certainly every other animal

87

in the world must have been afraid of him. There were dinosaurs like him all over the world for millions of years.

Tyrannosaurus Rex was 50 feet long, and his head was as high as three tall men, standing one on top of the other.

His teeth were as long as your foot. They had sharp, tearing edges, like the edge of a jig-saw blade.

The giant meat-eaters who lived earlier had weak little front feet which they used like hands. But the two-toed front feet of Tyrannosaurus were so weak and so small that he probably didn't use them for anything at all.

This monster was not only the largest, but also the last of all the giant meat-eating dinosaurs.

Other Cretaceous Animals

The last dinosaur period had more animals of all kinds than the earlier periods.

Now there were giant flying reptiles and big new swimming reptiles. And there were more kinds of snakes and turtles and lizards and crocodiles than ever before.

There were new kinds of insects, and there were birds almost like the birds we know. (They still had teeth, though, like their reptile ancestors.)

The mammals were small and weak, but they were larger than the mammals that lived in the Jurassic period. One kind of mammal was very much like an opossum; there were others something like a hedgehog.

There were still not very many mammals, but there would be more of them as time went on.

The end of the dinosaurs

In each of the three dinosaur periods, there were more dinosaurs than in the period before. Some kinds did die out, but there were always more new kinds to take their place.

But by the end of the Cretaceous period, every single kind of dinosaur died out. There were no more dinosaurs.

No one is sure why this happened.

Perhaps the world became too cool. (But other warm-weather reptiles, like the crocodiles, managed to keep on living.)

Maybe the world became too dry. (But then what about the dinosaurs who lived on dry land anyway?)

Some scientists say that the little mammals ate up all the dinosaur eggs. (But others think there weren't enough mammals to do this.)

The truth is that no reason seems to be exactly the right reason.

The truth is that we just don't know why all the dinosaurs died out.

There are many other things we don't know about dinosaurs. You will notice as you read this book that we often have to say "perhaps" or "we think" or "maybe" or "possibly."

We don't know all the places that dinosaurs lived.

We don't know how long a dinosaur lived. Was it a hundred years? Two hundred? Some people think it may have been even longer than that.

And why have we found so few fossils of *young* dinosaurs?

And did dinosaurs make any noise? Did they roar like alligators? Squeak like lizards? Whistle? Bellow? Scream? Moo?

And were all dinosaurs born from eggs?

There are many, many questions, and we may never know the answers to some of them.

But some of our questions may be answered tomorrow, or next year.

Many of the answers will surely be found by the time you are grown up.

Maybe you can help to find some of the answers yourself.

Index of dinosaurs

Scientists who study dinosaurs have divided them into two large groups, called *orders*. The dinosaurs of one order are called *saurischian* (**saw-ris**-kee-an) dinosaurs. The dinosaurs of the other order are called *ornithischian* (**or**-ni-**this**-kee-an) dinosaurs.

The bones around the hips of the saurischians are shaped very differently from the bones around the hips of the ornithischians.

If you plan to learn more about dinosaurs, you will want to know which dinosaurs were saurischians and which were ornithischians.

Look at the index of dinosaurs on pages 94 to 96. All the names printed in color are names of saurischian dinosaurs. All the names printed in black are names of ornithischian dinosaurs.

Index of dinosaurs